Italy

To the outsider, Italy is looked upon as the land of *la dolce vita* – the good life. It is a country famed for its cars, cuisine, culture and clothing. But behind this pleasant facade lies a nation beset with many serious social and economic problems, not the least of which is the continued division between the "rich" north and the "poor" south. The latter has been neglected for centuries and remains an area of peasant farmers, high unemployment, and little modern industry – a world far-removed from the bustling, industrial north. Today, firms are being encouraged to move to the south, transport facilities are being improved, and farming methods modernized; but the changes have not been fast enough to stem the trend of emigration, both to the north and abroad.

In *We Live in Italy*, a cross-section of the Italian population tell you what their life is like – life in a city, life on a farm, and life in industry.

The author, Tana de Zulueta, is a freelance journalist and broadcaster. She lives in Rome.

we live in
ITALY

Tana de Zulueta

A Living Here Book

The Bookwright Press
New York · 1983

Living Here

First published in the United States in 1983 by
The Bookwright Press, 387 Park Avenue South,
New York NY 10016
First published in 1982 by
Wayland Publishers Limited, England

ISBN: 0–531–04690–7
Library of Congress Catalog Card Number: 83–71635

Printed by G. Canale & C.S.p.A., Turin, Italy

Contents

"Union members are in a minority"

Mario Andreucci, 44, works on the production line at the Fiat car factory in Cassino, 130 km (81 miles) south of Rome. Mario is also a shop steward for the metal-workers' union.

I was one of the first men hired to work in this factory when it opened in 1972. Now there are 10,000 people here. Most of the workers come from the surrounding villages. This used to be one of the poorer areas of Italy, with small peasant farms and little else. The factory was built here to provide much-needed jobs and to bring industry to a backward area.

Moving straight from working in the fields to a big impersonal factory was difficult for many of the new Fiat employees. Some thought that a factory job would be a piece of cake, only to find themselves having to struggle to keep up with the conveyor belt and remember their assigned task.

As a union we try to handle workers' complaints by making requests to the management: trying to get an easier pace of work for our members, and generally improving working and safety conditions in the factory.

Mario presides over a meeting of the Cassino branch of the metal-workers' union.

The factory is one of the most modern in Italy. A lot of the more repetitive or dangerous tasks are now done by robots. As a union we're all in favor of these improvements, but we're worried that one day robots will be taking jobs away from the men and women who need them.

Union membership is optional in Italy. I've read that in some industries in England only union members can be employed – what they call a "closed shop." We've nothing like that in Italy. In fact, here at Fiat, union members are in a minority.

Nonetheless, the metal-workers' union is one of the most powerful in Italy, with its members in the most important industries, including automobiles, steel, shipyards and light-engineering companies. We can mobilize an impressive number of people. I remember a metal-worker's march in Rome when 50,000 strikers marched through the streets under their different banners.

We were marching to demand our new contract, which was months overdue. Every three years the union negotiates a new standard contract. This establishes basic pay and terms of employment for metal-workers throughout the country. The other big unions, like the chemical and textile workers, do just the same. As a result a worker in Cassino gets the same basic pay of 768,000 lire ($525) a month, five weeks' vacation and an extra month's pay a year, as a car worker at the Fiat factory in Turin.

The union takes up a lot of my time, both inside and outside the factory. Shop stewards are allowed by contract to take care of union matters, like planning meetings or drafting reports, during working hours. We also have our own meeting-room in the factory. About once a month a group of us travel up to Rome to attend

The Fiat factory at Cassino has provided 10,000 jobs in a backward part of Italy.

meetings at our union's headquarters.

I try to keep up with local problems, too. Because it's the only big factory in the area, everything in Cassino seems to revolve round Fiat. We try to press the bus company to adjust its timetables to suit Fiat employees, and we badly need nurseries where women can leave their children during factory shifts.

We've been worried recently by the temporary lay-offs at Fiat. Last week several hundred men were sent home on eighty percent pay, while the company tried to sell off surplus cars. Car factories all over the world have problems these days, not just in Italy, but if Fiat should stop providing jobs here at Cassino, we've not much else to fall back on.

"Ninety percent of Italians are Catholics"

Father Tolmino Zocchi is a parish priest in Rieti, in central Italy. Besides looking after his parish, he teaches religious education in the local middle school and coaches a junior basketball team.

I was ordained a priest by the Bishop of Rieti when I was nineteen, having studied in the Rieti seminary, a college where Catholic priests are trained. I was a bright child and my parents sent me to study in the seminary when I was ten. In those days it was the best way to give a village boy a good education. My parents also hoped that ultimately I'd take holy orders, and I didn't disappoint them. Now I cannot think of a better life.

Today, however, boys begin at the seminary when they're fourteen years old, or even later – it's never too late to hear the calling to become a priest.

I never lost touch with my home village of Leonessa, 40 km (25 miles) from here. I began taking groups of children from there on camping holidays as soon as I was put in charge of a parish. Later I founded a young people's holiday home near Leonessa. Children come from as far afield as Rome, particularly convalescent children in need of mountain air.

I get up at 5:30 or 6:00 a.m., then go to church to meditate. At 7:00 I say an early morning Mass, and at 8:00 I read my breviary – the book from which Catholic priests recite set prayers every day.

Father Zocchi is the coach for the junior basketball team of his parish.

At 8:30 I'm ready to take my classes at school. A weekly hour of religious education is compulsory in Italian state schools, unless parents ask for a special dispensation. The official religion in Italy is Catholicism. That is not surprising, since the pope, the head of the Catholic Church, lives in Rome, and ninety percent of Italians are baptized Catholics.

When I've no morning classes, I make my parish calls, visiting those who are too old or sick to move around. I try to keep in touch, not to let anyone feel forgotten; but it's not easy in a parish of 1,000 inhabitants – roughly 300 families.

This is a fairly average size. We have some bigger parishes, and many smaller ones. People have come down to the plains to work, and some mountain parishes have been almost abandoned, with only fifty parishioners left.

My parishioners take turns inviting me to lunch. I live alone, and though someone comes in twice a week to clean my house, I do my own cooking. Actually I've become quite adept at turning out a dish of bean and pasta soup, one of my favorites.

On most afternoons, and especially Saturdays, I teach catechism classes in church, instructing children in the principles and mysteries of the Catholic faith. I also hold regular meetings with the parish catechists, the men and women who teach catechism besides myself. Then at 6:30 p.m. I say another Mass.

After an early supper of milk and crackers, or bread and cheese, I hold parish meetings. Once a week we hold a meeting of young people between the ages of fifteen and twenty. I also make a point of talking to the parents of children preparing their First Communion. In Italy it's customary for children to take their First Communion when they're eight years old.

In his spare time Father Zocchi likes to play boccie. He's the neighborhood champion!

This is a very important date in a child's life: he or she becomes a full member of the Church, and it's a first step to growing up.

9

"Top-quality beef is a Tuscan specialty"

Domenico Micheli, 38, runs a butcher's shop in Cortona, a picturesque walled town of 22,650 inhabitants in southern Tuscany. He devotes most of his spare time to his dogs, a gun dog and guard dog, both champions.

I started this job when I was fourteen years old. It was my own choice: my father would have been glad to let me continue at school, but I thought working would be easier than studying.

Three times a week I'm up at 4:30 a.m. to get to the local meat market and make my choice of sides of beef, veal and pork. I also stock rabbits and poultry — chickens and turkeys. By 7:30 a.m. every day I have to be back at the shop to prepare the morning's display for opening time at 8:00.

I also buy my meat from the local slaughterhouse, then cut it up myself. I used to work with my father, but now I run the shop single-handed. I was worried for a while when they opened a supermarket nearby: with their pre-packed meat they were undercutting the prices of us traditional butchers. But I soon realized that people stick to a reliable butcher who provides good meat, well-cut and prepared before their eyes. The only kind of ready-made food I sell is dog food.

Top-quality beef is a Tuscan specialty. We have a local breed of cattle called

Domenico sells a variety of meat in his shop: from T-bone steaks to pig's feet and tripe.

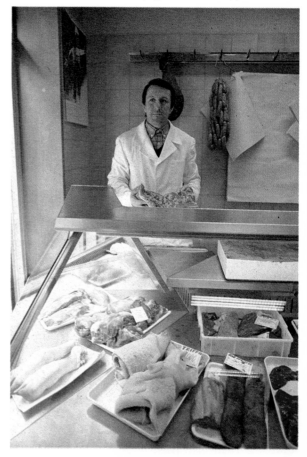

Chianina, named after the nearby Chiana valley, which provides the best steak of all. The traditional cut is the T-bone steak, known as the *Fiorentina*, or Florentine steak. It's cut an inch thick, and eaten grilled; one steak can easily feed two people. But at 13,000 lire a kilo ($4.00 a pound), hardly an everyday dish.

I sell a lot of poultry, and here, too, customers seem to go more and more for the quick and easy cut. Chicken and turkey breasts, for frying, sell so quickly that I stock boxes of just breasts, as well as whole birds. The difference in price is considerable: chicken breasts cost 8,400 lire a kilo ($2.60 a lb); while the best whole chicken only costs 2,500 lire ($1.70).

Most of our meat in Cortona is raised and killed locally, but nearly forty percent of Italian meat, with the exception of chickens, is imported. People are wealthier and their habits have changed. In my father's day most people in this area ate meat once a week; now a slice of meat at lunch and supper is quite normal.

I often wish I had more time to spend with my wife and two daughters. I close the shop at 8:00 p.m., then close the register and store the meat in the refrigerator. It's nearly nine by the time I get home.

Still, if I had to start all over again, I don't think I'd choose a different career. You see university graduates, who've spent ten years studying, looking for work. On the other hand, craft workers and tradespeople like me can live more than comfortably these days, so long as they're prepared to work. My shop brings in 44,000,000 lire ($30,000) a year, before taxes.

When I was a boy I'd often go hunting on weekends with my father. Game in Italy is public property, not the property of the landowner, and you can go hunting in most places, so long as you keep at least 100 meters (328 feet) from houses, and don't damage any crops. The hunting season lasts from September to January for most animals, and up till March for migrant birds. Unfortunately, now that most people can afford a car and a gun, many birds have become very scarce.

Domenico and his champion dogs, Bimbo, a Breton spaniel, and Saba, a German shepherd.

"People are eating fewer eggs now"

Angellina Colazzi's family has been farming the same fields in Umbria, central Italy, for 150 years. Angellina is a widow, and runs the farm with the help of her son, Alberto, his wife, and her youngest daughter.

Ours is a fairly small farm, about 25 hectares (6 acres) in all. Milk and eggs provide our regular income. Our six cows produce 180 liters (317 pints) of milk a day, for which we get 64,000 lire ($44). And we have 500 chickens. It's hard-earned income, though. We add cattle feed to our own hay, and the feed gets more expensive every year; while the price of milk remains low. Nor is it easy to find buyers for our eggs, because people are eating fewer eggs now. We sell a few in my son-in-law's shop, but we have to take the rest to market.

We sell the milk to a company in Perugia, which processes and pasteurizes it before distributing it around the town and throughout the province.

The company is run by the Perugia town council, and there are similar companies in all the main Italian towns. We have a contract whereby the company buys up all our produce. If the company has more milk than it can sell on a particular day, it processes it and sells it as long-life milk instead.

I get up at 4:30 a.m. in the summer to milk the cows and clean the stable, although in winter I can sleep until 6:00. We milk by hand; with six cows a milking-machine wouldn't be worthwhile, and besides I'm used to the milking.

When we've finished with the cows and chickens, we go to work in the fields. In the summer we're often there all day: early in the season there's the hay to be cut, dried and stored. We have planted a crop

Sugar beets are among the crops that Angellina grows on her farm in central Italy.

After milking her cows, Angellina has to clean out the cowshed.

of sugar beets this year. We also grow vegetables to sell in the market: beans, peppers and eggplant. Alberto studied at the agricultural college in Perugia, and although my husband used to say book-learning is no help to hill farmers, Alberto knows which pesticides to use. Two years ago he covered the vegetables with plastic sheets in the spring, and we made a good profit by selling them earlier in the season than other farmers.

We also have twenty-five sheep, which a local shepherd pastures for us, together with those of two of our neighbors. He is one of the few who still know how to make good seasoned sheep's cheese. My son-in-law sells our cheese in his shop in Perugia at 8,000 lire a kilo ($2.50 a pound); the tourists, he says, just can't get enough of it.

When all goes well, each cow gives birth to one calf a year, which we sell for meat for 600,000 lire ($410). Besides vegetables and livestock, we produce wine and olive oil, just for our own use. We have our own tractor, which we bought with a government loan, and Alberto also works our neighbors' fields with it for a fee.

People from the cities are buying old farms around here and converting them for weekends and vacations. A lot of old farms on the poorer land on the hillside have been abandoned for years: the owners went off to Perugia to look for an easier way to earn a living.

A Roman lady said to me the other day that country life is so much better than the rush and bustle of town. I'm used to it, but I don't think she'd like cooking dinner for seven hungry mouths after working all day in the fields.

"Long distance trips are easier and quicker nowadays"

Alberto Granaglia has been driving trucks for thirty-three years. Seven years ago he started his own transport business in Trecate, near Novara. His son and daughter help run the firm.

I learned to drive in the army. Looking back at the trucks we drove thirty years ago, I think life has become a good deal easier for truck drivers. Now we have power steering, power brakes, smooth gears and soundproof cabs. You no longer need a strong pair of arms to steer a heavy truck around the bends of our mountain roads.

One of my first employers was an international haulage company in Turin. I used to drive their trucks to and from France, Germany, Holland and Belgium. Eighty-six percent of Italian goods travel by road – more than in most European countries.

One of Alberto's trucks using an expressway. Tolls for trucks are expensive – up to 20,000 lire ($14).

The Italian railway network keeps a lot of us in business: it's so antiquated that on some routes, particularly to the south, a truck gets there in half the time – and time, of course, is important, particularly with a load of perishable goods. All the fruit of southern Italy – grapes from Apulia, peaches from Naples and oranges from Sicily – is rushed north by road.

We used to drive very long hours in this business, sometimes both day and night. But union rules and Common Market regulations have set a driving limit of eight hours a day. Owner-drivers, like me, regularly used to break this rule to make more money. Now it's not so easy to do, because a machine called a tachograph has to be installed in every truck's cab. This registers the driver's hours of rest and the time he spends at the wheel.

Long-distance trips, like the ones I used to make, are easier and quicker nowadays, thanks to expressways and the new tunnels under the Alps. Our expressways, or *autostrada* as we call them, are rightly famous. In mountain country it's an impressive sight to see the viaducts, which carry them, spanning the valleys.

Although, on many trips, expressways have cut traveling time by up to a half, not all truck drivers like to use them. Many, especially owner-drivers like myself, try to avoid paying up to 20,000 lire ($14) in tolls. Then there are other disadvantages: expressway restaurants, or *autogrills*, are expensive; and their bathrooms aren't designed for truck drivers: after a long day's driving you need a high, wide wash-basin to comfortably strip off your shirt for a real wash.

The little family-run restaurants off the expressways provide all we need: a shower, really good home cooking – with local wine to wash it down – and a landlord who'll take a telephone message from your wife if you're a regular customer.

I set up my own trucking business seven years ago. I was working for a company which sold heating oil and tractor fuel to small firms and rice farms in the Novara valley. The owner of the firm sold me two trucks, and "Granaglia and Son" came into existence. Both my ex-boss and I have benefited: he contracts with me to deliver his fuels, and knows that it's in my interest to make as many deliveries as possible – and I'm my own master.

Now that I've paid all the instalments on the trucks, we're doing pretty well. But we work hard: six days a week, and for long hours. We've built our own house on the edge of town, and my daughter is moving into another next door.

Expressways, like this one through the Apennine mountains, have cut travel times.

"At thirty-four I still hadn't qualified"

Fabrizio Frisardi opened his own architect's studio in Rome in 1981. He has been tied up ever since with the biggest project of his career: a prince's villa in Qatar. Fabrizio has a wife, Manuela, and a baby daughter.

I knew I wanted to be an architect from the day I left school. I was eighteen and had specialized in art and art history. My father didn't approve: he wanted me to study something more practical. He was an airforce officer and hoped I'd follow in his footsteps. It would have been a considerable sacrifice for him to send me to the university, so I looked for work right away.

I did odd jobs. They were often fun, and I was learning all the time. I illustrated children's books, and worked as a draftsman in architects' and interior decorators' studios. I even worked for a few years as a film-set designer after winning a grant to the Rome film school. I got my diploma there when I was twenty-three.

All this time I was studying at night to pass my architecture exams at Rome University, where I'd signed on as a student. Luckily, there's no time-limit for getting your degree. You just take the exams when you're ready. I must have been one of the slowest students ever!

I was making most of my money as an interior decorator. This was a step towards becoming an architect. The film director Bruno Corbucci was my first customer, and one order led to another.

As I progressed through my architecture course, I began taking on more ambitious work, doing such projects as restoring country houses or converting apartments.

But I had a problem: I had plenty of

The Frisardi family often goes for walks in the gardens of the Villa Borghese in Rome.

Fabrizio's biggest project yet: the plans of an Arab prince's villa in Qatar.

experience, but at thirty-four I still hadn't graduated. So I took a drastic step: I quit my decorating business and became a full-time student for a year. In 1977 I qualified as an architect. However, it wasn't a good moment for a completely unknown (and by now completely broke) architect to launch himself on the market.

The boom years were over and the Italian construction industry was almost at a standstill; even the most renowned architects were looking for work. I began with freelance work: small jobs and consultancies for big offices. The busiest offices were those with contracts abroad, particularly in the Middle East. Dozens of Italian firms are making money these days with building and construction contracts in oil-producing countries. So I looked for work there myself.

On a trip to Saudi Arabia for one of my employers, I learned that the Minister of Defense of the tiny kingdom of Qatar was commissioning a new house for himself. A prince's villa is more of a palace than a house, and the project was coveted by the biggest architecture firms in Europe. I returned to Rome and began to prepare a project to submit to the prince. I was confident that it was a good, attractive design; but it still seemed like a miracle when my plan was accepted. Maybe the prince liked it because I didn't doll up the villa with fancy domes and arches to make it look "Arabian." I designed a building I'd be happy to live in myself.

It's been a busy year. With a commission on this scale, I've had to hire outside help. Three of us have been working all out for eight months, and in a matter of weeks we'll be starting to construct the villa in Qatar. The prince has paid the first installment, so my wife and I are seriously thinking of buying the apartment we are renting. It's in the center of Rome.

" Training to stay at the top is hard work"

Sara Simeoni became a world-record holder in the women's high-jump in 1978. In 1982 she won two more international championships. Sara was born and lives in the village of Rivoli Veronese, near Verona.

I entered my first sports competition when I was thirteen years old, and won the high jump. Before that I was more interested in ballet. When I was eleven, I won a place at the ballet school of La Scala, the Milan opera house, and the best dance school in Italy. But my parents wouldn't let me go there.

When I was twelve I tried for an audition to dance with the corps de ballet in *Aida*, the opera composed by Verdi. It is performed every year in Verona's Roman amphitheater. But I was turned down because I had big feet and was too tall. I was terribly disappointed, and it was many years before I could get over it.

It was my gym teacher who first realized I might put my big feet and long legs to good use. One day she took me out into the yard and got me to jump a rope. I didn't have running-shoes, but I cleared 1.28 meters (4ft 2in). I won my first competition by jumping 1.30 meters (4ft 5½in), and setting a new record for my age group.

I joined a local sports club, but it closed almost immediately. Then our parents

First, again! Sara is congratulated by her trainer and fiancé, Erminio Azzaro.

all got together and founded *Scala Azzura*, the club I belonged to until I was eighteen. I was lucky. Many Italian children never do any athletics at school, and everything depends on being spotted by a good teacher. Often there aren't any sports fields where one can train. It's even harder for girls: sometimes there are no women's dressing rooms at local sports arenas.

When I could jump 1.80 meters (5ft 9in), it was time for me to move on. I was accepted by a club run by Fiat, the Turin car company, and the next year became Italian high-jump champion and ranked number ten in the world.

But my home town meant a lot to me, and I wanted to compete for Verona. So I joined a local club, hoping that people would begin to show a real interest in sports, but in Verona in 1973, athletics was taken about as seriously as birdwatching. Neverthless, I remained with a Verona club until I was twenty-five. By that time I was second in the world behind Rosemarie Ackermann, the first woman to jump 2 meters (6ft 6in).

In 1981 I was signed on by Fiat OM Brescia, another athletics club sponsored by Fiat. Nowadays the most important clubs are sponsored by major companies, and with their help and that of the Italian athletics federation (FIDAL), our top athletes are adequately supported.

Training to stay at the top is hard work. I'm lucky, as my trainer, Erminio Azzaro (ex-Italian high-jump champion), is also my fiancé, so all my achievements are doubly satisfying.

In 1982, I won two international championships, although I was laid up twice. I was unable to join in the European championships because of an inflamed tendon in my foot. But I still hope to improve my world record. Erminio and I feel I've got the potential to do so.

When I do retire – and I think it'll be quite soon – I intend to settle at Rivoli Veronese, where Erminio and I already have our own house. Erminio lends a hand with the grape harvest – grapes which my father turns into the best wine I know. I'd like to live a very quiet life: maybe we'll start a family, or open a sportswear shop, or I may even go back to teaching sports – who knows?

Another record jump for Sara? (Her best jump was 2.01 meters (6ft 7in) for a women's world record.)

"Italian circuses are famous in Europe"

Luciano Bello, 33, works as a clown with the Medrano circus company, one of the best known in Italy. He lives with his wife and their sons in a comfortable trailer, in which they have traveled around much of Europe.

Actually, I became a clown overnight. My father used to be a wonderful clown. He designed his own costume, and had his own style. Then one day he fell ill and they called me on at half an hour's notice. I put on his costume, copied his make-up and staggered out under the lights. I was terrified, but when I realized everyone was laughing, I was off and running.

When my father died six years ago, I took over his act permanently. Then I devised my own jokes, and added acrobats' tricks, which I'd been doing since childhood. I still wear a copy of my father's costume to carry on the family tradition.

We circus people are very close. Relatives all park their trailers next to each other, travel in convoy, help out with the chores, the children, and the repairs.

My wife Ioset is the daughter of the owner and manager of this circus. She and her sisters used to do an acrobatic-cycling act before they got married – all three married circus people. Now Ioset takes care of the household and the children. I wouldn't like my wife to have to work.

She's glad to lend a hand, though, helping out with the sale of tickets at afternoon and evening shows.

Our sons, Ronnie and Steve, attend classes in the circus's own school trailer. It's just like an ordinary school, with a blackboard, benches and desks, only it's mobile. The schoolteacher travels around with us: she says it's more exciting than being stuck in one place.

In the afternoons the kids start learning

The Bello family in their trailer home, which has taken them around Italy and Europe.

The end of another performance by members of the Medrano circus.

our trade under the big top. It's not a bad life for children. Work and play are one and the same thing for them. They're so used to playing in the big top that they grow up quite fearless.

In the summer the circus calls at seaside resorts on the Adriatic Coast – places like Rimini and Cattolica – and on the Tyrrhenian Sea, the west coast. Our family has traveled all over Italy with the circus, even to the islands of Sicily and Sardinia. We've also toured Spain and Greece.

Italian circuses are famous in Europe, and we produce excellent circus equipment. There's one company from Verona, near our home town of Bussolengo, which designed a mobile, self-raising frame for circus tents. The poles are powered by their own motors, and it's an impressive sight watching the big top rise smoothly up, apparently of its own accord.

A circus like ours provides jobs for 350 people. My earnings are reasonable. Although we live in trailers, we fit them out with all modern conveniences. Our own trailer has a shower, stove, refrigerator and parquet floor. We carry the extra luggage in our truck, where I've also installed a washing machine.

Circuses are fairly profitable businesses, but their running costs are very high. We use an enormous amount of electricity for lighting. Then there are wages, and social security payments. And you can imagine how expensive it is feeding lions and elephants! An elephant eats 100 kg (220 lbs) of hay a day, plus 20 kg (44 lbs) of oats and bran, apples, and sugar. We spend 700,000 lire ($480) a day on feeding our elephants. We spend 1,500,000 lire ($1,000) a day on the other animals. Consequently circus tickets aren't cheap: from 4,000 to 12,000 lire ($2.75 to $8.25) for adults, and half price for children. Our big top seats 3,500 people. There are dozens of small circus companies in Italy, but only about half a dozen can compete with us.

21

"In Turin the automobile is king"

Diego Novelli, 50, is the mayor of Turin, an industrial city of over one million inhabitants, and the capital of the Italian automobile industry. Before being elected mayor, he was a journalist for twenty-four years.

I was born in Borgo San Paolo. Then it was a neighborhood on the edge of a small town of 5,000. The old apartment houses were built round courtyards where we used to play. Our parents were poor, but all the families in the building knew one another.

This community feeling was destroyed when thousands of immigrants from the poorer south of Italy, where industry is scarce, poured in after World War II to find work at Fiat. The auto industry was booming, and in twenty years Turin swelled to four times its original size. The

Diego uses a helicopter to inspect new housing development in the suburbs of Turin.

fields which ran right up to the edge of the town vanished under rows of shoddy cement blocks.

Immigrants were crammed into apartments where no one knew anyone else. Transportation was lacking. Children went to school on alternate days because of the lack of classrooms. The historic center of Turin fell into decay as buildings became tenement apartments.

I became familiar with all these problems when I was still a reporter. Later I went into politics, but I went on writing about local problems until I ran for mayor in 1975.

I always tell people, "Don't expect miracles from me!" When I took over, the town hall was so deeply in debt, we could hardly pay our employees' wages. But I was determined to make Turin a better place to live in.

Large factories, and the automobiles they produce, are necessary; but our towns shouldn't exist just for cars. In Turin, where factories like Fiat and Lancia are the biggest industries in town, the automobile is king. But a town should be built for its inhabitants. Nobody, for example, had bothered to provide for the needs of children and old people.

One of my first projects was "Children's Summer," a project to reach tens of thousands of children. In an industrial city like Turin, both parents often work. Children were left on streets for most of the summer vacation. The project allows children to join groups in supervised activities. The whole city is put at their disposal, from the local TV station, to the firehouse, the police station, and the museums. We even arrange visits to a farm: a lot of town children don't realize milk comes from cows, and think it's made in a factory!

Situated at the foot of the Alps, Turin is an important industrial center, particularly for automobiles.

I receive 15,000 letters a year, a lot of them from children, and I answer them all. I've made many friends on my visits to schools, and some of them come and visit me at home, or bring over a decorated tree at Christmas.

In the past few years we've laid down traffic-free bicycle tracks, opened new public gardens, planted trees, organized concerts and exhibitions. Now there are day-nurseries in every neighborhood and enough classrooms to go round. We've still got plenty of problems, but I think people understand we're doing our best to solve them. Maybe the children who are four now will be given a chance to live in better surroundings and grow up differently from those who are already fourteen.

"Full-time school is still optional"

Marisa Boissi is a teacher at a junior highschool in Scandicci, a small town on the outskirts of Florence. Marisa lives in Florence, where her husband is a doctor.

I'm one of the two history, geography and Italian teachers for our ninth grade pupils. I teach one group of thirteen and fourteen-year-olds in Italian for five hours a week, and another in history and geography. As in all state schools, our classes are co-eds, and none of them goes over the legal limit of twenty boys and girls to a class.

Because it's the summer term, my pupils are already preparing themselves for their exams in June. Many of them think of the junior-high exam as a major hurdle, but few children actually fail. We prefer not to let a pupil take it who is unlikely to pass. Children who have done poorly during the year are expected to repeat the course, rather than go on to a highschool unprepared.

On the day of the exams, the class will take written tests in Italian, mathematics or science, and in the foreign language they have studied – at my school we offer English, French and German. English is the most popular.

I'll prepare the three written questions for the Italian language exam and I'll also mark my pupils' exams in history and geography. Both of these subjects, together with art and art history, are tested in an oral exam by a panel of teachers, including one outside examiner. We've been instructed this year to make our questions interdisciplinary – that is, to put questions to the children which are related to all the subjects they have studied. This takes a bit of effort when you're used to teaching each subject separately, but it can be very interesting.

Our school has switched over to a

Marisa's class joins tourists on a visit to the Loggia Della Signoria in Florence.

Marisa with one of the classes she teaches at the school in Scandicci, near Florence.

morning and afternoon schedule, as opposed to just morning, for nearly half the pupils. Full-time school, as we call this system, is optional: many parents still prefer to keep their children at home in the afternoons.

Our junior high curriculum consists of nine subjects: Italian, science and mathematics, history, geography, art, religious education, gym, and technical education. Technical education includes a number of applied skills, ranging from electricity to carpentry, needlework and photography. For each subject we have a set number of hours in which to complete the year's course of study: two hours of art a week, six of math and science, and three of technical-education, for example. Now, with afternoons at our disposal, we have the time to try interdisciplinary projects, as well.

This year the art teacher and I took our classes on outings to Florence. We could hardly have a richer field to study. Indeed, in Florence there are half a dozen museums, like the Uffizi, full of unique art treasures, and so many old churches and historic buildings to visit, one hardly knows where to begin.

Florence became the artistic capital of Europe in the fifteen century, largely because of the wealth of its merchants and bankers, and the skill of its craftsmen and weavers.

The third year of middle school is a child's last year of compulsory education. At fourteen you can leave school, if you wish. So I try to teach my pupils not just the facts in the curriculum, but also to help develop their critical understanding of the world in which they live.

Junior highschool teachers like me earn fairly average salaries: after ten years of teaching I earn 760,000 lire ($520) a month, after taxes. However, we have very generous vacations: two months in summer, and another two weeks at Christmas and Easter, which gives me a chance to spend some time with my son Gabrielle.

25

"The study of viruses is a fascinating field"

Professor Geo Rita has been the director of the Rome Virus Institute since its opening in 1969. During the forty-six years of his career, Professor Rita has witnessed some important developments in Italian science and medicine.

Like most of the teaching staff at the Institute, I began my career as a doctor. I got my degree in 1935 and went on to specialize in microbiology – the study of micro-organisms – in its medical applications. My teachers at Rome University included some of the most eminent Italian scientists of the day.

My first research was on infant diarrhea caused by bacteria. This was a very widespread problem in Italy in those days, particularly during the summer. Together with a colleague, I succeeded in demonstrating that these "summer tummies" were not due to eating the wrong things, as people supposed, but to germs in the babies' food and drink.

My research was interrupted briefly by the war, when I was drafted into the army. However, after a year I received a big surprise: my professor notified me that he had applied to the military high command to have me detached from my regiment to work on important medical research back in Rome.

My studies in microbiology gradually became more specialized. I gained my first professor's post at the University of Siena, in Tuscany, and spent the following seventeen years studying viruses. We worked on various types, including one which causes stomach upsets, and another which, like the polio virus, affects the

Professor Rita with one of his team of laboratory assistants.

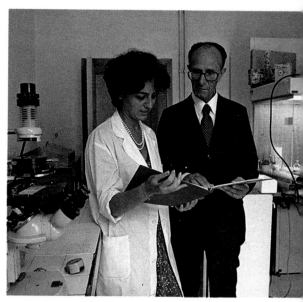

nervous system. Our aim was to find a vaccine against these viruses.

In my field you are sometimes fascinated by a brand-new discovery. You have a hunch that it could be terribly important, and if the hunch is confirmed, you can be repaid handsomely.

In 1957 British researchers identified a substance produced by living cells, which they called "interferon." I realized it was one of the most important discoveries of my era. Interferon is a substance produced by cells which stops viruses' multiplying. By immediately following up the discovery of interferon with researches of our own, my institute in Siena was able to contribute to the international study of this fascinating substance.

Nowadays the pharmaceutical industry world-wide has spent more than $500 million on researching the medical applications of interferon in the hope that it may provide a cure for cancer. But interferon can also be used to help us find out more things about how cells function.

Our institute here in Rome is relatively small but we're among the hundreds of researchers around the world working in this complex, but fascinating, field. Nowadays scientific progress is the result of good teamwork.

Unfortunately, I'm no longer able to devote as much time as I'd like to laboratory work. I arrive at the institute at 8:00 a.m., and a large part of my day is taken up with administration. I also lecture and organize laboratory sessions for students. Virology, which is the study of viruses, is an optional course in our faculty, but 200 students apply to take the exam every year.

Luckily, I'm an early riser: in order to do my own writing, I have to get up at around 5:00 a.m. I was born and raised in the country, in a village near Viterbo, north of Rome. My father was a primary-school teacher. As a printer in his spare time, he earned some extra money to bring up his six sons. My mother died shortly after I was born. By the time I reached school age, my father had the money to send me to a boarding school, and then to a university.

I married during the war, and my older three children have long since married and left home. The youngest, a social anthropologist, still lives with us. Next year I'll retire from being director of the institute, which will leave me more time to cultivate my hobbies: music, gardening, and archaeology. Actually, if I had to start all over again, I think I'd choose to be an archaeologist.

The Virus Institute, of which Professor Rita is the director, is part of Rome University.

"We're Sardinians first and Italians second"

Marta Puddu lives in a new apartment in Cagliari, the principal town on the island of Sardinia, with her husband Gavino and their two children. Gavino manages the Fiat showroom in the center of the town.

From our windows I can see the sea and the port. The view is what I liked best about the apartment when we moved in seven years ago. I come from Alghero, on the opposite, north-west side of Sardinia, where my father was a fisherman; so I was born and bred near the sea.

Looking after the children, fetching them from school, cooking and household chores take up all of my time now. I worked as a secretary in an insurance office before I got married.

Now I haven't time to get bored. I'm up before 7:00 a.m. to prepare breakfast – milk, coffee, bread and jam for everybody – before taking the children to school at 8:00. Lessons start at 8:30. It's not far to the

Lunch is served! Marta's mother-in-law helps her to prepare meals for the family.

school, just five blocks. But the morning traffic is terrible, so I prefer to see my children across the roads. By the time I get back, Gavino has shaved, had his coffee and set off to work.

I quickly clean up the breakfast things and make the beds, before doing the shopping. I buy most of our food in the municipal market, a covered building with every kind of food stall: fruit, vegetables, cheese, meat and fish. They even sell flowers there. The prices are better than in the stores, and the food is fresher. I'm a regular customer at one of the stalls, but I still look around to compare the prices.

We have splendid fruit and vegetables in Italy, but food gets more expensive every year, especially meat, fish and cheese. We all love fish at home, but I never buy it. We wait until my father comes to visit us with an icechest of bream and red mullet – the choicest fish of all – and we have a little feast.

I enjoy cooking, but I'm fussy; if I make meatballs in sauce, I like to grind my own meat. For lunch I usually prepare pasta – the children love it – and some meat, then fruit. We always have wine (for the grown-ups), and water and bread on the table. When my mother-in-law gives me a hand with the cooking and ironing, I find time to make our favorite dessert, a Sardinian speciality called *sebadas*: fried pancakes stuffed with fresh white cheese and eaten hot with honey.

Two afternoons a week the children go back to the school for optional activities: painting and English lessons for Irene; painting and sports for Mario. When they stay at home they play in the yard between ours and the neighboring apartments which means that somebody has to keep an eye on them, especially on little Mario. Gavino and I finally have a little time to

Marta buys most of her food from stalls in the municipal market at Cagliari.

ourselves after supper, when we watch television and I knit.

We both regret there are so few local television programs. We Sardinians are proud of our traditions. We speak our own dialect. When a Sardinian travels to the mainland, he says he's going to "the continent." Nowadays, because of school and television, everybody here speaks perfect Italian. We have adapted our life style, but we're still Sardinians first and Italians second.

29

"We're having to lay off 200 workers"

Carlo Ottolenghi is the manager in charge of industrial relations with one of Italy's leading domestic-appliance manufacturers. Born in Rome, he now lives with his wife and two sons in Fabriano, central Italy.

This is the problems department. What we do in this office is cope with all the little hitches which crop up in a company with a work force of 2,000 in five factories, scattered all over Italy. As soon as I get in at 8:00 a.m., the phone rings, and it doesn't stop until I pick up my coat to go home at six in the evening.

This morning, for example, they called me from our factory near Naples, in the south of Italy. We're having to lay off temporarily 200 workers there, as the demand for our dishwashers is decreasing.

The workers are obviously afraid the lay-offs will be permanent, and this morning they started to picket the gates: nothing can now be brought in or out of the factory and we can't deliver to our customers. Oh, we certainly have plenty of worries these days!

This company makes washing machines, refrigerators, dishwashers and kitchen units. Last year this was still a booming industry. People were buying Italian appliances all over Europe. Our British rivals were worried about an "invasion" of

Italian washing machines. But the market has become overcrowded. We have five large and very aggressive competitors in Italy. In times of economic difficulties people try and make do without new machines, hence our present difficulties.

My problems, of course, have to do with people, not the machines they produce.

Will people buy these washing machines after they've been assembled?

Dealing with the problems of 2,000 workers means that Carlo's office is a busy place.

This morning I went down to the factory to attend a workers' meeting. The biggest grumble was the canteen service: not enough variety, they said, and the first course was always overcooked. They argued that the food served to the employees here in the administrative building is far better. I suppose the problem is it's easier to cook for 50 than 500.

However, we must take their suggestions into consideration. I do all I can to avoid strikes. In Italy last year more than a hundred million hours were lost because of strikes. But with a little tact one can avoid a lot of trouble. Actually I get on quite well with most of the trade union leaders, the men I have to negotiate with almost every week of the year.

The workers call me *dottore* (doctor), which is the polite way to address university graduates in Italy. All of my colleagues in management are graduates too; not one of them has worked his way up from the shop floor. Signor Antonio Ferro, the owner and chairman of the company, is the one exception. He and his father started off with a tiny company making water-heaters in a shed behind their house.

Our clerical staff in Fabriano are local people, but a lot of our engineers, designers and managers are from Turin and Milan, the cities in the north of Italy with the best industrial training schools. These colleagues are outsiders like me. We enjoy working here – the company is very dynamic, and the work challenging – but we all miss our home towns.

"The fish don't stand much of a chance these days"

"Don" Gennaro Guida is a fisherman from Gaeta, a seaside resort and fishing port 100 km (62 miles) north of Naples. "Don" Gennaro is 71, but he still takes his wooden row boat out into the bay almost every day.

I was the youngest of a family of eight. My father was a fisherman and I learned my trade from him. I've been fishing these waters since I was seven years old, except for the five years I spent in the army during the last war.

When I was a young man, a fisherman who owned his boat and knew his job could live decently and bring up a family on what he caught. I used to catch up to 80 kg (176 lbs) of fish each day, single-handed. Now the sea is so depleted, I'm glad to bring in a tenth of that!

Some say the fish have been killed by pollution from the industrial wastes and detergents which run into the sea from big towns like Naples.

I don't think the fish stand much of a chance these days. When I take my boat

"Don" Gennaro with fellow fishermen. They call him "Don" out of respect.

out in the summer I see more divers in their wet suits than fish. The divers shoot the fish with spear guns in their dens and in the holes in the rocks we fishermen can't reach. We were brought up to throw an octopus with eggs back into the sea, but these people take whatever they can get.

Besides divers, there are the big fishing-boats, and there are more of them than in the old days. Small-boat owners like me can't compete with these large boats. They have crews of five men or more, and are equipped to stay at sea for days, with refrigerated holds to store their catch. They're built for fishing on the high seas, and it's illegal for them to come in closer than 3 km (2 miles) from the shore. But I've often seen them fishing on the sandbanks near the coast when they know there's fish to be found. By combing the seabed with their drag nets, they destroy the areas where the fish breed.

Here in Gaeta we fish mainly with nets. I use a piece of net 700 meters (2,297 feet) long, weighted with lead, which I cast in shallow water. The net sinks to the bottom and is held vertical by its floats, forming an invisible barrier in which the fish get caught. I put my net out just before sunset, casting it in the places near rocky shoals where I know fish will pass. Then I come back before dawn to haul it in. I often manage quite a decent catch: some squid, maybe a few prawns, grey mullet and, best of all, red mullet – a small, but prized fish.

At my age, though, hauling nets is heavy work, and if my nephew isn't around to lend me a hand, I usually prefer trawling with lines. On a good day I might land a couple of bream, which can fetch 15,000 lire a kilo ($4.60 a pound). That's how it is: I catch less, but I'm paid far more for what I do catch, and somehow I get by.

I never married, but I brought up my two

Away from the sea, "Don" Gennaro cultivates the vegetable patch at his home.

orphaned nephews. The younger married and left five years ago, but my nephew Gaetano still lives with me. Feeding his four small children is almost more than he can afford, so, old as I am, I still go out to work. Because I never made social security payments when I was young, I can only draw a minimum pension: 300,000 lire ($205) a month. Luckily I enjoy fishing. Everyone knows me down on the seafront: they call me "Don" out of respect.

"A year in the army is compulsory"

Carlo Mazzoni is studying law at Milan University. Like most Italian students, he is attending the university in his home town. Milan is the second largest city in Italy, and the country's business capital.

I bicycle to lectures almost every day. I was brought up here and I'm used to the traffic and the bustle. Of course I could take the subway, but I prefer making my own way across town. And besides, cycling is a way to keep fit.

The university is a big place, the second largest in the country, with faculties offering courses in all subjects. Most of the university buildings are gathered together in a large compound known as the "city of studies," on the east side of Milan. During weekends the alleyways between buildings are crowded with students – some would say too crowded. On some mornings I've found myself struggling to find a seat in a lecture hall packed with 500 people!

Higher education in Italy is open to anyone with a high-school diploma, which accounts for the numbers, especially at the major universities. I believe this is right, because it gives everyone a chance for higher education. But it does cause problems. About 80,000 men and women graduate from Italian universities every year, which means, of course, that my

Carlo is in his final year at Milan University. Here he studies for his graduation exams.

degree will by no means guarantee me a job. In law, alone, there are about 7,000 new graduates every year! Still, with my final exams coming up at the end of the year, I can only keep my fingers crossed.

It has taken me five years to complete the course – longer than the normal four years of a university degree course, but you must allow for the fact I took a year off to do my selective service. A year in the army is compulsory for men in Italy. I had an easier time than most, because, instead of being confined to the barracks, I swam for the Italian Army team. Training in a swimming pool was probably more fun than doing drill on the parade ground. Now I'm helping to pay my way through the university by giving private swimming lessons in a club in the suburbs.

Not that the university fees are high, just 100,000 lire ($68) a year. But then there are books, clothes, and general living expenses: all of which are a considerable burden to my parents, with three of us still living at home.

When I graduate I hope to enter the judiciary service. This means taking a very stiff entrance exam, but if I succeed, after a two-year training period, I will become a magistrate, a member of a corps of 7,000 judges attached to the hundreds of courts in all the main Italian towns. This is a position of real responsibility, whether one works in the civil or criminal courts. It should also be a very interesting job, as Italian magistrates don't just judge cases in court, they also direct police investigations into all reported crimes. Our legal system is based on ancient Roman law, which was substantially modified and improved by Napoleon in the eighteenth century.

If I do succeed in becoming a magistrate, like most recruits, I'll almost certainly be sent to a small local court possibly right

Carlo helps to pay for his education by giving private swimming lessons.

at the other end of the country. I have spent all my life in Milan; it will be hard to leave, even though people from the south tease me about the weather here always being foggy and gray.

"In Rome they often put beds in the corridors"

Maria Zanon has been a nurse for fifteen years. She is a staff supervisor in a state hospital in Piacenza, a busy city of 109,000 inhabitants, in northern Italy. Italy has many private clinics, because of the poor facilities in state hospitals.

I start work at 7:00 a.m., and the first thing I do when I arrive is drink a cup of strong, black *espresso* coffee. Then I settle down to my job: coordinating the nursing staff and assigning them to the different wards. We have several nuns working as nurses here, as in most Italian hospitals, and quite a few male nurses. Then there are the nurses' aides and the hospital orderlies.

This used to be a private clinic, before it was passed over to the local authorities. Now it's part of the Italian national health service, but it is administered locally by the regional government.

There are still many private clinics in Italy; not surprisingly, because I must admit that Italian hospitals are not always what they should be. In cities like Rome the wards are so overcrowded that they often have to put beds in the corridors. But staying in a private clinic can cost 112,500 lire ($77) a day – not for all pockets!

When I've checked who's absent and found replacements, I report to the hospital director. After completing my administrative tasks, the nurses will tell you that I bother them all morning. Why were the windows left open? Why isn't the surgery floor mopped? But that's my job – I am paid to supervise others.

The nurse-ranking in Piacenza hospital: nurses aide, nurse, and staff supervisor Maria.

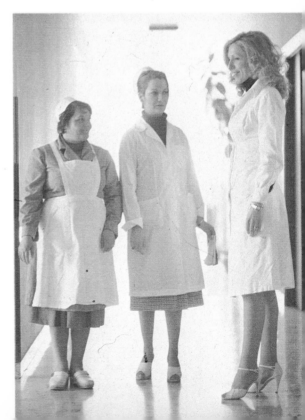

The hospital where Maria works. It was originally built as a private clinic.

If a doctor needs anything from the nursing staff, he asks me first. I also work in the operating theater, as nursing coordinator, and sometimes I actually assist the surgeon. I do that for love, because we have strict rules as to what each person is qualified to do; but, like most Italian hospitals, we are chronically short-staffed, and the fact is I have more practical experience than most of the nurses – and many of the young doctors. So in an emergency I often find myself passing the doctor what he needs before he even asks for it. On top of all this I was elected the representative for the hospital workers' union last year.

As you can imagine, time flies by. At 2:00 p.m. I have lunch – the same lunch as the patients – and more coffee, and my day is over. Unless, of course, there's an emergency and I have to rush back. I work six days a week and, like most people in Italy, I get one month's vacation a year, but can only take two weeks at a time. I used to go back to Trieste – where I was born – with my mother. But this year I'll be going to a holiday camp in Sicily with my fiancé and another couple.

After work I look after my mother who's not very well. If I have time, I play tennis or go to the movies. In the evening I like to go out dancing with my fiancé. My favorite club is the "Paradiso," where there's a good floor show; they serve dinner and you can dance as well. My fiancé wants me to stop work when we marry, but I won't. I'm unusual, as most girls give up their jobs when they marry.

"Naples is the home of the pizza"

Tano Barbuto works as pizza cook in Amalfi, one of Italy's most picturesque seaside resorts. Tano is 31, the oldest of five children. He lives with his family in a three-room apartment in the old part of the town.

My first jobs were seasonal ones: helping out in restaurant kitchens during the summer months. In winter I often didn't earn any money for weeks on end. I did all sorts of jobs: washing dishes, waiting on tables, and chopping vegetables. I left school when I was fifteen and began working as a pizza cook five years later. I learned this job in a restaurant on the main square. There I helped the cook during the peak hours to shape the pizzas before baking. But it wasn't till I was in charge myself that I really knew what to do.

Every pizza cook has his own recipe. Nobody taught me mine: I worked it out for myself. I don't weigh or measure the quantities. I use a large tin can for the water, and work out the proportions by eye: roughly speaking, one liter (two pints) of water absorbs two kilos (four and a half pounds) of flour. I measure the salt by the fistful, and put in just enough oil to give the dough a slightly shiny look – all pizza cooks add some fat because it makes the dough crisper.

I still do everything by hand. There are pizza restaurants where the dough is kneaded mechanically, and the cheese is grated by machine. But where I work it wouldn't really be worth it, and besides, I think pizzas taste better when made by hand. I knead the dough myself, and

Tano uses a special shovel to put a pizza into the wood-burning stove's oven.

Tano's pizzas are piping hot when they are served to hungry diners.

crumble the cheese to sprinkle on top. We use mozzarella cheese, a speciality of this part of Italy. The best mozzarella is made of buffalo's milk, and the taste is superb. But real buffalo-milk cheese is too expensive for cooking, so we use mozzarella made from cow's milk instead.

Nowadays all restaurant-owners are on the lookout for a good pizza cook. That is why, once you're established and the owner knows customers are coming in because they like your pizzas, the pay isn't bad. I make 900,000 lire ($616) a month.

I work eight hours a day, from 4:30 p.m. until 12:30 at night. I prepare the evening's dough as soon as I arrive, leaving it to rise in a large tub in the kitchen. Then I light the fire. The best pizza is made in a wood-burning stove, which takes an hour to heat up to the correct temperature – and longer if the wood doesn't burn well. Pizzas are served in the evenings, which means pizza cooks, unlike waiters and the rest of the kitchen staff, don't work in the mornings.

Things really begin speeding up at around 8:00, when couples start strolling in from the main square, looking for a bite to eat. In summer, when the hotels are packed with tourists, the orders come in faster than you can clap your hands. Every customer wants a different pizza: with or without anchovies; with mushrooms, or ham, or olives; or all three, plus an egg. Naples is the home of the pizza and the traditional Neopolitan pizza is plain cheese and tomatoes, and this is the base for all the other variations.

Working in front of an open red-hot oven takes some getting used to. In summer, when the weather's warm as well, I'm soon drenched in sweat – but too rushed to wipe if off! The hours aren't easy either: I'm never in bed before 2:00 a.m. And we work on public holidays too, including Christmas and Easter.

Now that I've acquired the skill, I'm going to be a pizza cook for the rest of my life, but one day I'd like to have my own restaurant in Naples.

"We sell 300,000 copies each day"

Giancarlo Baccini is a journalist on the Rome daily newspaper *Il Messagero*, which has the highest circulation of all the city's newspapers. He has covered four Olympics, and every world tennis championship since 1971.

I went from playing sports to sports writing. I played water polo for ten years, writing sports items part-time for *Il Messagero*. Then I got married and soon had to give up water polo: journalism and family life were taking up all my time.

I get into the office at 10:30 a.m. with a stack of newspapers under my arm. Then I compare our coverage to the other papers. By mid-morning we start planning tomorrow's paper. The first list to be drawn up is the sports section – a priority, I tell my colleagues, because the sports pages are what most of our readers look at first.

After the morning editors' conference, I make phone calls and contact our correspondents until lunch time. Things really get moving in the afternoon: short of an emergency we know what the next day's paper will look like at the 4:30 conference. Late-night surprises are fairly rare in sports, as all the events are scheduled.

One evening we'd got both the sports pages laid out early, so I said to my pals as a joke, "all we need now is a world record." And sure enough at 8:45 the

Tomorrow's paper takes shape: Giancarlo attends the morning editorial conference.

Italian high-jumper Sara Simeoni broke the world record at Brescia. The printers were all set to run the page at 9:00 and the whole department went into a panic.

Actually we can go on adding important news items until 1:30 a.m., but the first edition closes at 10:00 p.m. *Il Messagero* runs a "national" edition, but in practice the paper is only distributed in the Latium region around Rome, and the provinces just beyond. Altogether we sell 300,000 copies each day, which means we have the highest circulation in Rome and the third highest in Italy. Three hundred thousand copies may not sound like much. In some countries, there are newspapers that sell a million copies a day. But even the newspaper with the highest circulation in Italy, the prestigious *Corriere Della Sera* of Milan, only sells 500,000 copies. We Italians are notoriously poor newspaper readers. The only papers to actually make a profit are the sports ones.

Editing and layout, which we call "kitchen" work, have changed completely with the introduction of new computer technology.

The owners of *Il Messagero* (our shareholders are a group of large industrial companies) decided to introduce the new technology in 1980. In many ways it was welcome, being so much faster and more flexible, but it puts dozens of printers' jobs at risk. Consequently there was an uproar at the paper. The printers went on strike during the 1980 Moscow Olympics, and the paper didn't come out for days. Then the printers' union finally agreed to phase out eighty jobs. Some of those workers took early retirement.

Luckily my job isn't all office work, and I still do plenty of reporting. My specialties are swimming, tennis and, of course, water polo; but we're flexible: when I started I

Sports papers and magazines sell quickly from news-stands in the streets.

wrote about rugby and baseball, both of which are beginning to catch on in Italy. I never miss the Davis Cup tennis finals in the United States, and I love my annual trips to London to cover Wimbledon.

41

"We never meet the people who apply for jobs"

Angelo Valente, 40, works for the local education authority in Naples. He is an actor in his spare time and has now established himself as one of the best-known amateurs in Naples.

Like many young men from the south of Italy, when I got my law degree at Naples University, I applied to join the Civil Service: there weren't many other alternatives for graduates. I decided to join the police force and, after taking the entrance exam, I was appointed a police inspector. Then I took a four-month course at the police officers' training college in Rome.

When this was over, I was sent to Pordenone, a town in the northeast of Italy.

I could hardly have been farther from my home town, Naples. I only went home twice a year. I was appointed chief of the

Angelo (second from the left) is an actor with the "La Paranza" theater group.

local crime squad. It was a busy and exciting job, but my father didn't approve. "The cop," he used to call me. He wanted me to go back to Naples and have a more conventional job.

He got his way in the end. I came home and joined the local education authority. I clock in at 8:00 every morning – one of the 500 employees in this monster office. I'm head of the section where applications for non-teaching jobs, such as janitors, secretaries and technicians, are graded in order of merit. I have eleven employees working under me, each with his specific task. But I regard them more as colleagues than subordinates.

Each day in the office is much like another. I've been here for nine years, and every year seems just like the one before. We have our office rituals: such as the mid-morning break at the canteen on the ground floor – a chance to exchange gossip with acquaintances from other departments. We have no lunch break: like all civil servants, we work from 8:00 a.m. to 2:00 p.m., then knock off for the day.

Frankly I preferred being a policeman. I'd arrive at the station every morning without ever knowing what might happen, or when I'd get to bed that night. I was constantly in touch with reality: criminals, their families – the reality of the dramas in these people's lives. Sometimes, even, men and women from the criminal underworld would turn to me to help them start a new life.

Now, instead of people, I deal with bits of paper. Behind every application there's probably some personal tragedy, like a man with a family to support who has just lost his job. But we can only assign jobs on a points system, taking into account seniority and qualifications. We never meet the people who apply for jobs.

As soon as I returned to Naples I began to take an interest in the theater, and in poetry. I once heard that every Neapolitan is a poet at heart. I've written poetry all my life, some in Italian, some in the Neapolitan dialect. A collection of my poems has been published. There are nearly thirty small publishers in Naples, producing about 300 books a year in the Neapolitan dialect.

It was a short step from reading and writing poetry to acting. I began with an amateur group: we'd hire a theater for a couple of evenings, or put on a show in a disco before it opened at night. There are dozens of companies like ours in Naples.

I was one of the few actors to go beyond the amateur circuit. I've played in professional theaters in Naples, and with national companies, as well. But I act for the pleasure it gives me: I'd hate to depend on it for a living.

Angelo is head of the section which deals with non-teaching jobs in the Naples area.

"Girls don't live alone in Sicily"

Gabriella Minucci, 28, is an artist. She lives in a top-floor studio apartment on the Via Marguta in the heart of old Rome. There are many artists in the area, and the street is lined with art galleries.

On my passport-application form this year I was able to put artist as my profession. Getting there wasn't easy though. I was born in Agrigento, on the south coast of Sicily. I'm very fond of my home town, but it has no art galleries and no art school, and painting was always my great passion.

I went to the university in Palermo, a two-hour drive from my home, and studied in the literature department. I was particularly interested in local literary traditions: theater and poetry written in Sicilian dialect. Meanwhile, I was doing small paintings for myself and for my friends.

Now I paint mainly traditional religious scenes on wooden tablets or pieces of glass. I do this to revive a dying Sicilian tradition. I met my boyfriend on a trip to Rome two years ago to attend a conference on popular art. He works as a draftsman, and when he saw my paintings, he said he was sure people would buy them. He introduced me to a gallery owner who liked my work and asked to see more. I was terribly excited: a month later I was back in Rome with a suitcase-full of my painted tablets.

Then the gallery owner did something fairly unusual. He offered his gallery, here on the Via Marguta, for a personal show, in exchange for a percentage of the sales.

Gabriella painting a picture of an archangel on a piece of glass.

44

Most artists exhibiting their works in this street are established figures in the art world: the unknowns sell their work on trestle tables out on the pavement. "It's a gamble," the owner told me. But it worked, and I haven't looked back since.

I sell my work at prices from 80,000 to 500,000 lire ($55–$350), depending on the size. If you take a look at the galleries round here, you'll see far higher prices. But I get lots of orders now. This year I've been commissioned to do an altarpiece for a new church. I will decorate a piece of glass 10 meters (33 feet) long to stand behind the altar: it's my biggest project yet. Decorating churches is one of our oldest artistic traditions. It goes back to the Middle Ages.

I'm studying art restoration here in Rome to learn some of the old techniques, like how to use gold leaf. Gold goes very well with the vivid colours I use.

Gabriella's studio apartment is decorated with examples of her paintings.

I do most of my painting at night, when I'm at my best. I paint until 4:00 or 5:00 a.m., and then I get up very late. But as soon as I'm up and washed, I pick up my brushes and only stop for a sandwich for lunch. In the evening my boyfriend comes 'round and we have dinner and gossip with our friends – painters, art critics, or gallery owners – in the little restaurants, called *trattorias*, in our neighborhood.

My parents used to worry about my living alone in a big city. Girls don't live alone in Sicily: we're still very traditional down there. But now that they see I've made a name for myself, they're very pleased. Like all Sicilians, though, they value the family more than anything else, and wish I were with them more often.

"Most people cannot afford brand-new cars"

Vincenzo Costanzo is 16 and still new to his job in a body shop, repairing the damaged bodywork of vehicles and re-painting them. Vincenzo lives and works in the historic city of Bologna.

I've been working here with Sergio Angeli, my boss, for just over a year now. We get on well – he's a friend of my dad – but we work hard. As soon as I arrive at 8:30 in the morning, he gives me some task to do. But we don't pull up the steel shutters and start attending to customers until 9:00 a.m.

I didn't know a thing about painting cars when I first arrived, but Sergio says I've learned fast. My dad says Sergio is one of the best in the business. We're so busy that we often have to turn customers away. We paint and repair some splendid cars. Sergio says you read in the papers that the country is going broke, but the cars seem to get bigger every year. When he started his business twenty years ago, he hardly ever saw a foreign car. There were very few luxury cars, just the occasional Alfa Romeo, from the Italian company, famous for its fast cars. Now we see a lot of new imported cars, but not Japanese ones. Sergio says that if the Italian government lifted its import restrictions on Japanese cars, we would see them everywhere, because they're cheaper than our Fiats. But most people cannot afford brand-new cars: the average age of cars on the road is eight years, which also shows what good mechanics we must have!

I wanted to be a car mechanic when I left technical college. I did odd jobs for a garage near my home, but the owner already had an apprentice. Then Sergio offered to take me on permanently.

The premises are small, and work often spills out onto the pavement.

It's not a bad job. Now that I know how to use the special oven for "baking" the paint onto cars, Sergio pays me 720,000 lire ($492) a month; but after taxes and social security, I take home 640,000 lire ($438). One day I hope it'll be a lot more. This is a profitable business, and who knows, maybe I'll be running a bodyshop of my own in a few years.

My mother is grateful for what I can pay to help with the housekeeping, but I've been spending most of what I earn. I've bought a motor scooter, a Vespa, and some new clothes. The Vespa was my big dream when I was still at school. I couldn't wait to leave and earn some money of my own.

I went to technical college when I was thirteen. We did the usual school subjects: history, Italian, math, as well as the technical courses. I liked the applied electricity course best. We had a great teacher

Vincenzo knows how to use the special oven for "baking" paint onto a car.

who started us on all sorts of projects. He even took us to the electric company's headquarters here in Bologna and showed us the electrical system at the town hall. It was fun, and now I can fix any electrical fault at home. Maybe it would have been more useful if I'd become an electrician, or even a mechanic. But finding work isn't so easy these days, and most of my friends are still without jobs, even though they've been looking for ages.

After work or on the weekends, I usually meet my friends 'round the corner. I scoot up on my Vespa and we chat or play pinball before going home for supper at around eight. Saturday night we all go off to the local disco. But most evenings I watch television at home with my family.

47

" The Carabinieri carry out police duties, but they are part of the Italian Army"

Salvatore Masciari was sworn in as a Carabiniere five years ago. He left his home in Campobasso, southern Italy, to train in Rome. Now he lives in barracks on the Via Garibaldi, one of Rome's most exclusive streets.

My first post in Rome was at the Vatican station near St. Peter's Square. I was only nineteen, but my superiors thought well of me, and I was put right onto sentry and patrol duty. With thousands of tourists and pilgrims passing through the square every day, we were ordered to watch for thieves and pickpockets.

Since his election in 1979 Pope John Paul II has kept the policemen and Carabinieri attached to the Vatican very busy indeed. The Pope was a very popular bishop in his home country, Poland, and he still loves to mingle with the crowd, which means that his public appearances are a terrible headache for the officers who organize his protection. There were hundreds of police and Carabinieri in St. Peter's Square on May 13, 1981, when the Pope was shot by a Turkish terrorist; but they were unable to prevent the attack.

The Carabiniere, who stopped the attacker under the colonnade in St. Peter's Square, is a friend of mine. I wasn't there that day, but we were called in from patrol on the outskirts of Rome to set up road-blocks and check the traffic heading out of the city: it was thought that the Turk might have had some accomplices, but we didn't arrest anybody.

I've been involved in many other anti-terrorist operations since I was transferred

Salvatore contacts his headquarters on the radio in his Alfa Romeo patrol car.

48

An anti-terrorist operation: a night-time road-check on Rome's ring road.

to the Rome mobile squad two years ago. The Carabinieri carry out police duties, but they are part of the Italian Army. Like any soldier, a Carabiniere knows he may often risk his life, but it's terribly difficult to get over it when somebody you know gets killed.

A hundred years ago our corps was used against the bandits who used to hide in the mountains all over Italy; now we are used to hunt out terrorists. Terrorism is a major problem in Italy these days. And just as the Carabinieri used to ride fast horses, now we drive the fastest Alfa Romeo sedan. We keep in constant radio contact with our command branch. Each car is manned by two, sometimes three, men. We run routine patrols, ready to dash to the scene of an emergency.

There are 85,000 men in the Carabinieri. We have operational units in all the main towns, and a network of local stations right across the country, even in the most remote country villages. There are also special squads of Carabinieri trained to operate in the open country or in the mountains, on skis or horseback if necessary.

This month I'll be taking a special exam. If I pass, I'll become a non-commissioned officer after a two-year training course. Then I'll be put in command of a patrol car or, if I leave the mobile squad, of a station. My salary, too, will improve. I shall apply to be transferred to near my home, Campobasso.

A lot of my colleagues are from the south of Italy. There's very little industry down there, so you don't have much choice when you're looking for a career. We used to joke when we were kids that if you wanted to find a job you either became a football star or joined the Carabinieri. I played on the Campobasso junior football team for a year, but I didn't make the first division – so here I am!

49

"Ivrea has remained an unspoiled town"

Gianni Ravani was born in Campiglia Soana, a village at the foot of the Alps, in northern Italy. He moved to Ivrea when he married twenty years ago. He has worked in the Olivetti factory there ever since.

My first job at Olivetti was making typewriters. A lot of things have changed since then. Olivetti doesn't make typewriters in Italy any more: the Olivetti typewriters you buy here are manufactured in Spain or Brazil. At the Scarmagno factory where I work, we make telex terminals and mini-computers.

Olivetti is a multinational company, making office equipment of all kinds: furniture, calculators, photocopiers and computer systems and, of course type-writers. To keep up with the times, the company has gone over to electronics in a big way – Olivetti engineers even invented the first electronic typewriter. All this has changed the factory where I work, with more and more specialized technicians taking over jobs. I started as a manual worker here, but by taking company courses, I'm now classified as highly skilled.

I work in the section making telex terminals. If you walk through our department you might be surprised to see a woman crocheting while other workers are busy at their machines. This is because we've been organized into production "islands": a group of workers is responsible for assembling and doing quality control on one unit within a complete machine. Each worker organizes himself as he pleases, as long as he finishes his task on time. I can work fast enough to find time to go to the bank inside the

Gianni plays in a band which takes part in Ivrea's annual carnival.

Gianni assembles a telex machine in the Olivetti factory at Scarmagno, near Ivrea.

factory, or if a lunch-hour card game lasts long than expected, we make up for it afterwards by working harder.

We're spoiled in many ways here at Ivrea. When I joined the company our boss was Adriano Olivetti, the founder's son. We used to all him Adriano, and he took care of his workers in a way no other factory owner did in those days. We had free medical care, nurseries for the children, and company vacations at the beach.

Now that they both go to high school in Ivrea, my two daughters, Claudia and Mirella, have taken to lunching in one of the company cafeterias. The cafeterias are open to all employees and their families. A choice of two pasta dishes, meat, vegetables, cheese and fruit for 675 lire (46¢) is a bargain anywhere these days, so you even see managers and their families eating there.

There's a company bus service which drops me almost at my front door, so I usually come to work by bus. The service was one of Adriano Olivetti's most far-sighted ideas: thanks to him, although

10,000 people work in the Olivetti plants around Ivrea, most live in their home villages, and Ivrea has remained an unspoiled little town of 28,000 inhabitants, without any sprawling industrial suburbs spoiling its character.

With the help of a company loan, my wife and I have renovated our house and built a garage. I'm thinking of taking up one of the early retirement plans the company is offering: with automation and electronics, Olivetti is cutting back on jobs.

I wouldn't mind retiring, now that my oldest daughter is all set to leave home and go to the Olivetti training school to learn to be a computer programmer. I'd probably find a part-time job as an electrician; then I'd have time to practice the trumpet. I play with a band in Ivrea. We're one of the attractions at the yearly carnival – a splendid event, with processions of townsfolk in medieval costume.

"We still don't get very much homework"

Sandra Testa is 10 and in her fifth year at primary school. Next year Sandra will move on to junior high. She lives in Genoa, a city of 800,000 inhabitants on the northwest coast of Italy, and a major port.

At 8:20 every morning the school bell rings and we all make our way up to our classrooms. There are twenty children in my class. Lessons begin at 8:30, so we prepare our notebooks and pens at our desks while we wait for our teacher, Signora Scansano, to begin.

After the latecomers have dashed in, Signora Scansano raps her ruler on her desk and says *"Buongiorno!"* (good day). We answer *"Buongiorno Signora!,"* then we all sit down. Today we began with history.

Our other subjects are Italian, math, geography and science. Twice a week I stay on after school ends at 12:30 p.m. for English lessons, with seven of my classmates. My parents would like me to learn to speak English, and maybe next year another foreign language as well, probably German.

My school is gradually changing over to a morning and afternoon timetable, instead of just mornings, like most Italian schools. But we don't yet have a school cafeteria, so I have to go home for lunch and come back for swimming, drawing and afternoon lessons three times a week.

At the end of the summer term we'll have to sit an exam before going on to junior high next year. There will be written tests in Italian and math. But Signora Scansano says that for history, geography and science we only have to answer oral questions on what we learned this year.

Ten-year-old Sandra is in her last year at primary school in Genoa.

Sandra prepares her classroom project on ancient myths at her home.

We don't have foreign language exams until we get to junior highschool.

Junior high will be very difficult. Here in primary school we still wear smocks in class, but next year we won't any more. My class is the oldest in the school now, and the first-grade children, who are only five years old, are still babies really. Signora Scansano says that next year we'll be the babies in the junior high, and maybe the older children will tease us, but we mustn't mind. Signora Scansano teaches us everything except English and swimming, but next year we'll have a different teacher for each subject. I think lessons will be more difficult in junior high.

We still don't have much homework to do. Sometimes we do a few exercises at school in the afternoons with a lady supervisor. Otherwise we are given projects to take home. I call up my best friend, Cristina, while I'm doing my homework, and we tell each other how we're doing. What I like best, though, are the group projects. Last week we finished one on mountain animals. Four of us prepared it together. We showed how some animals change their color in winter to hide in the snow; and we also drew and wrote down what they eat and where they live. I used my own science encyclopedia for that: I've one on plants and one on animals. We've also just done a project on ancient myths. We studied Romulus and Remus, the twins who founded Rome.

On wet afternoons on weekends I sometimes go to the movies with Cristina and other friends, but we prefer to play outside. Mother often takes me and my baby brother Leo to the gardens at Nervi, a nearby village, or we go down to the little beach on the waterfront. It used to be forbidden to swim in the sea there, because all the sewage from the town and the factories dirtied the water. But they've built purifiers and the water is clean now, so in the summer we often swim next to the fishing boats down there.

Bruno Esposito, 20, lives in Naples. He got his accountant's diploma a year ago but, like many newly-qualified Neapolitan young people, Bruno is unemployed. He knows that Naples is the hardest place in Italy to find a job.

I don't have much to look forward to in the mornings, but I still try to make each day different. I get up early, particularly if the weather's fine, and make my way down to the seafront.

I usually meet my friend Massimo in a bar, and sometimes we buy the papers together – not the daily newspapers, but specialized publications like *Il Posto* (The Job), or *Il Concorso*, which lists all the government and local-authority jobs.

Like me, Massimo chose to go to a commercial accountancy school, which is one of the alternative types of secondary school in Italy. It's not an academic course, like the five years at a *liceo classico* (the name comes from the classical languages, Greek and Latin, which pupils learn). But in four years it prepares you for a range of clerical and accounting jobs.

Actually I don't think it's worthwhile trying for a *liceo classico*, though it's supposed to be the best type of school of all. My older brother Pasquale went to the local *liceo*. He's very bright, and now in his last year of studying political science at

Naples University; but he's so sure he won't find a job next year that he has already registered as unemployed.

Last week I registered at the employment bureau. There must have been seven or eight hundred people in line with me – the longest line in Naples! This year the local authorities have decided to take a census of the Neapolitan unemployed. According to official estimates, there are 110,000 people without a job in Naples, out of a population of 2.5 million. No other

Bruno earns a little money by playing the piano in a local theater.

The longest line in Naples: unemployed people register at the employment bureau.

city in Italy has such a high number of unemployed. In the area around Naples there are over half a million out of work.

There were boys with their diplomas straight from industrial training schools in the line with me; even qualified architects, as well as older men and women who must have lived by doing odd jobs all their lives. We Neapolitans are famous for having invented the "art of getting by." You see people earning money in the strangest ways: refilling disposable cigarette lighters instead of throwing them away; sewing up gloves at 500 lire (35¢) each; or selling smuggled cigarettes.

Cigarette-smuggling is big business here in Naples, particularly in my own neighborhood of Santa Lucia. The smugglers go 80 km (50 miles) out to sea, just beyond Italian territorial waters, to a waiting ship. They load up their launches with boxes of American cigarettes. The launches are the fastest models on the market, so they can outstrip the coast-guards' patrol boats.

I was once told that cigarette-smuggling provides a livelihood for 250,000 people in Naples! Maybe the coastguard knows this. Rather than starving out Santa Lucia – and driving people to even more unlawful ways of making a living – they seem to give the smugglers a sporting chance and don't really chase their boats.

I don't want to resort to that to make a living. My father sent us all to school to keep us off the streets. But I'm not very hopeful of finding work through the employment bureau. At least I'll be eligible, as of this year, to unemployment benefits of 200,000 lire ($137) a month.

There are four of us at home at the moment and we're all living off my father's pension from the railways. I'd take any job just to get some money, but this year I haven't even been able to get a waiter's job. The tourist season was bad, and the big hotels were half-empty. But what can I do?

55

"Tourism has been an important industry for years"

Paolo Guarducci mans a tollgate on the highway connecting Ravenna with the Bologna-Taranto highway. Paolo lives in a new house near Marina di Classe, a seaside resort just south of Ravenna.

I work for the Autostrade Company, the state-owned firm which built and now manages over half of the 5,900 km (3,666 miles) of Italian expressways. I've been doing this job for eight years, ever since the Ravenna expressway was opened in 1973.

It's not a bad job, and the hours actually suit me. I'm up before dawn to clock in at 6:00 a.m. if I'm on the morning shift. If I do the afternoon shift, I work until 10:00 p.m. The night shift is the hardest: traffic's scarce, and it's difficult not to doze off.

If I'm on the entrance booth, I issue the tickets to vehicles going onto the expressway. First I assess the size of the vehicle. I go by horsepower for cars, and capacity for trucks. Then I punch the information onto a ticket. The tollgate operator at the exit gate, say Milan, reads Ravenna as the point of entry, and feeds the ticket into a machine which works out the price. For a medium-sized car, the Ravenna–Milan journey costs just over 7,000 lire ($4.80).

The Autostrade Company uses the money it raises from tolls to cover the costs of the highways it has already built, to maintain them, and to build new roads. On some stretches of expressway, like the Florence–Pisa branch, there are automated tollgates: incoming drivers just press a button, and a machine provides them with a ticket. A special microwave "reader," which we call a banana because of its shape, has already assessed the size of the vehicle.

Automation is now being introduced gradually on the stretches of road with the heaviest traffic. We don't have a very heavy workload at this exit, as it isn't a through-road. But because of tourism, and its port and petrochemical plant, Ravenna was considered important enough to justify an expressway of its own.

The heaviest traffic on the A14 (short for *autostrade*, or highway, number 14) is just out of Bologna, with over 24,000 vehicles passing a day. This is a rich agricultural and industrial area, but traffic gradually falls off as you move south. The last leg of the A14 is one of the least-used expressways in Italy. This was a case of a highway being built more with an eye to developing an isolated and scarcely-industrialized part of the country, than to bring in immediate profits.

My brother has a small business at Marina di Classe, renting out deckchairs and changing cabins to tourists. In the summer I prefer to work nights on the expressway, so that I can help my brother during the day.

All in, including compensation for nightshifts, I take home almost 1,000,000 lire ($684) a month. We have no children, and my wife works in a local pottery

Paolo punches the point of entry and the size of each vehicle onto a ticket.

Paolo and his wife have bought a piece of land and built their own house.

factory, making tiles. Between us we've been able to buy a piece of land near the pine forest of Classe, and build our own house.

Along this stretch of the Adriatic, tourism has been an important industry for years, with resorts such as Rimini and Cattolica catering to tens of thousands of visitors. But this year the hotel owners are complaining that there were fewer foreign visitors than the year before. My company confirms this. According to the Autostrade Company, fewer cars passed through the highways leading into Italy in 1981 than in 1980. Prices have gone up and many tourists are going elsewhere – or not going on vacation abroad at all.

57

"Richer people don't seem to go out much"

Bruno Corbucci is one of Italy's most popular film directors. He has made thirty-three films, as well as writing plays. He lives in a big apartment in Rome, with his English wife and their two sons.

I only make comic films; mainly ones for kids between sixteen and twenty, because they're the only people who still go regularly to the movies in Italy. And it's definitely not a sophisticated audience: it's the theaters in the poorer areas on the outskirts of towns that are packed every night.

Richer people don't seem to go out much any more. Maybe they're afraid: there are a lot of robberies and kidnappings in Italy nowadays. The sorts of people who watch my films don't have those worries. They don't have much to lose and are tough enough to look after themselves. If you drive past the rows and rows of anonymous apartment houses in the residential areas around Rome, you'll see the kids sitting on the curb for lack of anything better to do.

The hero of the film we're making now is a bit of a rascal and speaks Roman slang. He wears a knitted cap covered in badges, jeans and a leather jacket. Tomas Milian, the actor, plays this rough-and-ready character that I invented.

Tomas has become quite a popular hero. The audiences of slum kids just love him – he's one of them, you see. Yesterday we were filming in Rome and in minutes there was a crowd of hundreds of boys around Tomas, all clamoring for his autograph.

These are difficult days for the Italian film industry: money is short. Take this scene we're filming now: our hairdresser

Bruno with the actor Tomas Milian, who has become popular with young movie fans.

UNO CONTRO L'ALTRO
PRATICAMENTE AMICI

ANNAMARIA RIZZOLI E CON BOMBOLO · SOGGETTO E SCENEGGIATURA DI BRUNO CORBUCCI · MARIO AMENDOLA · UNA PRODUZIONE INTERCONTINENTAL FILM COMPANY · COLOR TELECOLOR
UN FILM DI BRUNO CORBUCCI

A poster advertising one of Bruno's recent comedies, starring Tomas Milian.

and make-up lady is also playing a part, which accounts for the delay while she puts on her costume. Everybody lends a hand to keep the costs down.

I'm a quick worker, and that saves money. Every extra day's filming means a great deal of money: there's a crew of at least ten, then the actors, the extras, and the studio rent to pay for. But I usually only need to shoot a scene once, and in five to six weeks I've finished filming. All in all it takes me about four months to make a film. I complete about two films a year. In fact, I'm writing the next one on weekends.

Tempting people to go out in the evenings and leave their television sets is a hard job. The three state television channels show about one film a day; but the movies' biggest competitors are the thousands of local television companies which have sprung up since 1977, when private television was legalized in Italy. Nowadays, by switching channels, one can watch films nonstop, day and night. Here in Rome there are no less than thirteen local television stations.

The studios here aren't as glamorous as Cinecitta, Rome's world-famous studios, but they're quite adequate for us. And whatever happens we stick to union regulations about hours of work. In a few minutes we'll knock off for lunch. The leading actors go out to eat in a local restaurant, but I stay here for convenience. Technicians, the cameramen, an actor's agent, all sorts of people will probably want to talk to me. A film director has to coordinate a small army of people. I'll be lucky if I find time to call my wife at home.

59

"I serve about a thousand cups of coffee each day"

Nicola Primerano serves coffee in one of the best cafés in Rome. He began working in cafés when he was twelve years old. Nicola lives on the outskirts of the city with his wife and two children.

It's an hour-and-a-half by bus into work every day. I have to be in the café at 7:00 a.m. if I'm on duty for opening time at 8:00. We have to get the coffee machine started, the cups and saucers laid out, and sort out the rolls and sandwiches that the cooks begin to send up. I put on my uniform and white apron, then draw up the steel shutters to let in the crowd of bustling men and women on their way to work.

Most Italians drop into a bar at least once a day. Every day I serve about a thousand cups of coffee! Even when there are two of us behind the counter at peak hours, it's difficult to keep up with the orders. But with different customers pressing up against the counter every five minutes, we still manage to remember what each one asked for.

It's all a matter of practice. I was twelve years old when I started working in a café, near the station. It was very hard work, serving at tables and carrying trays of coffee round to the nearby offices from 7:00 in the morning until 10:00 at night — and all for 11,250 lira ($7.70) a month!

Things have improved a lot since then: with overtime and tips I take home about 1,000,000 lire ($684) a month — a fair enough sum! I would say this job is just like any other, and the long hours don't trouble me particularly. After seventeen years I'm used to it!

I don't feel particularly tired, but when I get home in the evening I prefer to stay in and play with the children, because I see them so little. Sometimes I help my wife in the kitchen, but I admit it's not often I do. She used to work as an analyst in a medical laboratory, but she gave that up when we got married four years ago. Even so the two children are a full-time job, and she only finds time to cook quick simple dishes: some spaghetti, a slice of meat, a salad.

We don't go out much. After all there are plenty of films on television. What I like watching most of all are the cartoons: I think I enjoy them more than my son does!

On my day off my wife and I often take the children into the center of town on the bus; we go for a walk in the park of the Villa Borghese, or around the Spanish

Italy is a nation of coffee drinkers. Nicola serves about a thousand cups of it each day.

Steps. My wife is Roman and so she's used to these beautiful places. She used to live quite near them when she was a girl, and before the rents became too high. But like most of the people living in Rome, I come from the provinces. My parents came here from Calabria, the region right in the southwest of Italy, when I was a boy, because my father couldn't find work down there.

This summer I'll be driving the whole family, including my parents, down to our home village. Most of the men there have to travel north to find work, many of them as far as West Germany and Switzerland, but they all come back in August. The village is very quiet for most of the year, but while we're there it's one long party for everyone, and we have a lot of fun.

When the café is busy, it is difficult to remember what each customer ordered.

61

Facts

Capital city: Rome.

Principal language: Italian. German is spoken in the Alto Adige region on the Austrian border. In the Basilicath region in the east, there is an Albanian-speaking minority.

Currency: The lire; 1,463 lire equal $1.00.

Religion: Roman Catholic. More than 90% of Italians are Roman Catholics. There are about 100,000 Protestants and about 50,000 Jews.

Population: 57,200,000 (1982). The country is densely populated. With 1.5% of the total area of the U.S.S.R., Italy has the equivalent of 22% of the U.S.S.R.'s population. There are eight large cities: Milan, Naples, Rome, Turin, Genoa, Florence, Palermo, Bologna. They contain 37% of the total population, but only occupy 4% of the total land area.

Climate: Mediterranean.

Government: Italy is a "democratic republic founded on work." The Parliament is composed of a Chamber of Deputies and a Senate. The Chamber of Deputies consists of 630 members, elected for 5 years by the country's voters. The Senate has 315 elected members and 7 life senators. The members are elected for 5 years on a regional basis, each region having at least 6 senators. The President of the Republic is elected in a joint session of the Chamber and the Senate for 7 years. The Council of Ministers holds executive powers. Reorganization of the Fascist Party is forbidden. Direct male descendants of King Victor Emmanuel are excluded from all public offices, have no right to vote or be elected, and are banned from Italian territory. The major political parties are: Christian Democrats, Socialists, Communists. Italy is divided into 20 regions *(regioni)*, 15 of which enjoy special status. There is a large degree of regional autonomy. Each region has a regional council which exercises legislative power, a regional government *(giunta regionale)* and a president of the government, which exercise executive power. Liaison between the regional bodies and those of the state is carried out by a commissioner of the government, who lives in the regional capital.

Housing: Government encouragement of home ownership has only been partially successful. Some houses have appalling sanitary conditions, particularly in the south of Italy.

Education: There are more state schools than private schools; the latter are usually run by religious bodies. Education is compulsory between the ages of 6 and 14. Schools' curricula are standardized by the Ministry of Education. There is an optional preschool education for children, aged 3 to 5, in preparatory schools. Primary education lasts for 5 years, between the ages of 6 and 11. Pupils have to obtain their lower secondary certificate to pass on to senior secondary education. Secondary schools *(scuola media)* open the way to art institutes, professional institutes, and technical schools. They also lead to schools which allow entry to universities. These schools, technical institutes and grammar schools *(licei)*, offer courses lasting 5 years. There are two types of *liceo*, one specializing in the classics, and the other in the sciences. There are many state universities and some independent ones, too.

Agriculture: 40% of the land is covered by mountains and plains and is often either too wet or too dry. Sufficient wheat is grown to feed the population; but most of the meat and dairy produce has to be imported. Main crops are: rice, wheat, corn, grapes and olives.

Industry: The country's industrial sector, particularly engineering and other manufacturing industry, is growing. State-owned industries account for 50% of total national industrial investment. The bulk of manufacturing output comes from small and medium-sized companies, mainly in the north and center of Italy. The textile industry is important, especially the production of artificial and synthetic fibers. Other important industries are: steel, cars and electrical appliances. In 1978 there were 20.5 million people employed and 1.7 million unemployed. The Southern Italy Development Fund *(Cassa per il Mezzogiorno)* was set up to develop the poorer, southern areas of Italy: to provide hospitals, communications, education, and attract industry. In northwest Italy, the average annual family budget was more than 19% above the national average, while in the south, Sicily and Sardinia, it was more than 23% below the national average.

The Media: Considering Italy's population, the number of daily newspapers is small: 72 dailies; 14 published in Rome and 9 in Milan. The dailies are entirely dependent on financial support from large industrial companies, political parties etc. All political parties in the Parliament have their own newspaper. There are 430 non-daily newspapers and 4,000 periodicals. The illustrated weekly papers and magazines have higher sales than the average daily paper; many of the former are sensationalist. There is no press censorship. Broadcasting is controlled by the state. There are 1,000 private local radio stations since a court case in 1975 gave citizens a right to free local information. There are 3 radio channels and 3 TV channels. There are over 9,000 movie theaters. Italy has made a great contribution to international film-making.

Glossary

Amphitheater An open-air theater, semicircular in shape, with seats in tiers around its sides.

Carabinieri Similar to state troopers; members of the Italian Army who perform police duties.

"Closed shop" An agreement between a labor union and employees, allowing only union members to work in a particular industry or factory.

Corps de ballet All the dancers of a ballet company.

Dialect A variation of national language spoken in one region of a country, or by one class of its people.

Immigrant A person who moves from his home region to another one, or from his home country to another one.

Magistrate A person concerned with the administration of the country's legal system.

Parish A district of a town or in the country, which has its own church and priest.

Pesticide A chemical used for killing pests which damage crops.

Pharmaceutical industry The manufacture or selling of medicinal drugs.

Shop steward A person elected by union members in a factory to speak on their behalf.

Sponsor A firm or person who finances something, often in return for publicity.

Tenement An often run-down apartment building, usually in a depressed area of a city.

Index